RICKY ROOGLE

PASSWORD LOGBOOK
FOR Am@ng.us FANS

THIS BOOK IS PROPERTY OF
NAME, FIRSTNAME:
STREET / NR.:
POSTAL CODE (ZIP) / TOWN:
PHONE:
EMAIL.:
NOTES:

Bibliografische Information der Deutschen Nationalbibliothek:
Die Deutsche Nationalbibliothek verzeichnet diese Publikation in der
Deutschen Nationalbibliografie; detaillierte bibliografische
Daten sind im Internet über http://dnb.dnb.de abrufbar.

© 2021 Ricky Roogle; 1. Auflage
Covergraphic, text & illustrations © 2021 Ricky Roogle
contact author: ricky.roogle@t-online.de

Herstellung und Verlag: BoD – Books on Demand, Norderstedt
ISBN: 9783752658217

TITEL:

WEB ADDRESS:

LOGIN / USER:

PASSWORD / PIN:

NOTES / RECOVERY QUESTION / PASS PHRASE / HINT:

AF237185

TITEL:

WEB ADDRESS:

LOGIN / USER:

PASSWORD / PIN:

NOTES / RECOVERY QUESTION / PASS PHRASE / HINT:

TITEL:

WEB ADDRESS:

LOGIN / USER:

PASSWORD / PIN:

NOTES / RECOVERY QUESTION / PASS PHRASE / HINT:

TITEL:
WEB ADDRESS:
LOGIN / USER:
PASSWORD / PIN:
NOTES / RECOVERY QUESTION / PASS PHRASE / HINT:

TITEL:
WEB ADDRESS:
LOGIN / USER:
PASSWORD / PIN:
NOTES / RECOVERY QUESTION / PASS PHRASE / HINT:

TITEL:
WEB ADDRESS:
LOGIN / USER:
PASSWORD / PIN:
NOTES / RECOVERY QUESTION / PASS PHRASE / HINT:

TITEL:
WEB ADDRESS:
LOGIN / USER:
PASSWORD / PIN:
NOTES / RECOVERY QUESTION / PASS PHRASE / HINT:

TITEL:
WEB ADDRESS:
LOGIN / USER:
PASSWORD / PIN:
NOTES / RECOVERY QUESTION / PASS PHRASE / HINT:

TITEL:
WEB ADDRESS:
LOGIN / USER:
PASSWORD / PIN:
NOTES / RECOVERY QUESTION / PASS PHRASE / HINT:

TITEL:
WEB ADDRESS:
LOGIN / USER:
PASSWORD / PIN:
NOTES / RECOVERY QUESTION / PASS PHRASE / HINT:

TITEL:
WEB ADDRESS:
LOGIN / USER:
PASSWORD / PIN:
NOTES / RECOVERY QUESTION / PASS PHRASE / HINT:

TITEL:
WEB ADDRESS:
LOGIN / USER:
PASSWORD / PIN:
NOTES / RECOVERY QUESTION / PASS PHRASE / HINT:

TITEL:
WEB ADDRESS:
LOGIN / USER:
PASSWORD / PIN:
NOTES / RECOVERY QUESTION / PASS PHRASE / HINT:

TITEL:
WEB ADDRESS:
LOGIN / USER:
PASSWORD / PIN:
NOTES / RECOVERY QUESTION / PASS PHRASE / HINT:

TITEL:
WEB ADDRESS:
LOGIN / USER:
PASSWORD / PIN:
NOTES / RECOVERY QUESTION / PASS PHRASE / HINT:

TITEL:

WEB ADDRESS:

LOGIN / USER:

PASSWORD / PIN:

NOTES / RECOVERY QUESTION / PASS PHRASE / HINT:

TITEL:

WEB ADDRESS:

LOGIN / USER:

PASSWORD / PIN:

NOTES / RECOVERY QUESTION / PASS PHRASE / HINT:

TITEL:

WEB ADDRESS:

LOGIN / USER:

PASSWORD / PIN:

NOTES / RECOVERY QUESTION / PASS PHRASE / HINT:

TITEL:
WEB ADDRESS:
LOGIN / USER:
PASSWORD / PIN:
NOTES / RECOVERY QUESTION / PASS PHRASE / HINT:

TITEL:
WEB ADDRESS:
LOGIN / USER:
PASSWORD / PIN:
NOTES / RECOVERY QUESTION / PASS PHRASE / HINT:

TITEL:
WEB ADDRESS:
LOGIN / USER:
PASSWORD / PIN:
NOTES / RECOVERY QUESTION / PASS PHRASE / HINT:

TITEL:
WEB ADDRESS:
LOGIN / USER:
PASSWORD / PIN:
NOTES / RECOVERY QUESTION / PASS PHRASE / HINT:

TITEL:
WEB ADDRESS:
LOGIN / USER:
PASSWORD / PIN:
NOTES / RECOVERY QUESTION / PASS PHRASE / HINT:

TITEL:
WEB ADDRESS:
LOGIN / USER:
PASSWORD / PIN:
NOTES / RECOVERY QUESTION / PASS PHRASE / HINT:

TITEL:

WEB ADDRESS:

LOGIN / USER:

PASSWORD / PIN:

NOTES / RECOVERY QUESTION / PASS PHRASE / HINT:

TITEL:

WEB ADDRESS:

LOGIN / USER:

PASSWORD / PIN:

NOTES / RECOVERY QUESTION / PASS PHRASE / HINT:

TITEL:

WEB ADDRESS:

LOGIN / USER:

PASSWORD / PIN:

NOTES / RECOVERY QUESTION / PASS PHRASE / HINT:

TITEL:
WEB ADDRESS:
LOGIN / USER:
PASSWORD / PIN:
NOTES / RECOVERY QUESTION / PASS PHRASE / HINT:

TITEL:
WEB ADDRESS:
LOGIN / USER:
PASSWORD / PIN:
NOTES / RECOVERY QUESTION / PASS PHRASE / HINT:

TITEL:
WEB ADDRESS:
LOGIN / USER:
PASSWORD / PIN:
NOTES / RECOVERY QUESTION / PASS PHRASE / HINT:

TITEL:
WEB ADDRESS:
LOGIN / USER:
PASSWORD / PIN:
NOTES / RECOVERY QUESTION / PASS PHRASE / HINT:

TITEL:
WEB ADDRESS:
LOGIN / USER:
PASSWORD / PIN:
NOTES / RECOVERY QUESTION / PASS PHRASE / HINT:

TITEL:
WEB ADDRESS:
LOGIN / USER:
PASSWORD / PIN:
NOTES / RECOVERY QUESTION / PASS PHRASE / HINT:

TITEL:
WEB ADDRESS:
LOGIN / USER:
PASSWORD / PIN:
NOTES / RECOVERY QUESTION / PASS PHRASE / HINT:

TITEL:
WEB ADDRESS:
LOGIN / USER:
PASSWORD / PIN:
NOTES / RECOVERY QUESTION / PASS PHRASE / HINT:

TITEL:
WEB ADDRESS:
LOGIN / USER:
PASSWORD / PIN:
NOTES / RECOVERY QUESTION / PASS PHRASE / HINT:

TITEL:
WEB ADDRESS:
LOGIN / USER:
PASSWORD / PIN:
NOTES / RECOVERY QUESTION / PASS PHRASE / HINT:

TITEL:
WEB ADDRESS:
LOGIN / USER:
PASSWORD / PIN:
NOTES / RECOVERY QUESTION / PASS PHRASE / HINT:

TITEL:
WEB ADDRESS:
LOGIN / USER:
PASSWORD / PIN:
NOTES / RECOVERY QUESTION / PASS PHRASE / HINT:

TITEL:
WEB ADDRESS:
LOGIN / USER:
PASSWORD / PIN:
NOTES / RECOVERY QUESTION / PASS PHRASE / HINT:

TITEL:
WEB ADDRESS:
LOGIN / USER:
PASSWORD / PIN:
NOTES / RECOVERY QUESTION / PASS PHRASE / HINT:

TITEL:
WEB ADDRESS:
LOGIN / USER:
PASSWORD / PIN:
NOTES / RECOVERY QUESTION / PASS PHRASE / HINT:

TITEL:
WEB ADDRESS:
LOGIN / USER:
PASSWORD / PIN:
NOTES / RECOVERY QUESTION / PASS PHRASE / HINT:

TITEL:
WEB ADDRESS:
LOGIN / USER:
PASSWORD / PIN:
NOTES / RECOVERY QUESTION / PASS PHRASE / HINT:

TITEL:
WEB ADDRESS:
LOGIN / USER:
PASSWORD / PIN:
NOTES / RECOVERY QUESTION / PASS PHRASE / HINT:

TITEL:
WEB ADDRESS:
LOGIN / USER:
PASSWORD / PIN:
NOTES / RECOVERY QUESTION / PASS PHRASE / HINT:

TITEL:
WEB ADDRESS:
LOGIN / USER:
PASSWORD / PIN:
NOTES / RECOVERY QUESTION / PASS PHRASE / HINT:

TITEL:
WEB ADDRESS:
LOGIN / USER:
PASSWORD / PIN:
NOTES / RECOVERY QUESTION / PASS PHRASE / HINT:

TITEL:
WEB ADDRESS:
LOGIN / USER:
PASSWORD / PIN:
NOTES / RECOVERY QUESTION / PASS PHRASE / HINT:

TITEL:
WEB ADDRESS:
LOGIN / USER:
PASSWORD / PIN:
NOTES / RECOVERY QUESTION / PASS PHRASE / HINT:

TITEL:
WEB ADDRESS:
LOGIN / USER:
PASSWORD / PIN:
NOTES / RECOVERY QUESTION / PASS PHRASE / HINT:

TITEL:
WEB ADDRESS:
LOGIN / USER:
PASSWORD / PIN:
NOTES / RECOVERY QUESTION / PASS PHRASE / HINT:

TITEL:
WEB ADDRESS:
LOGIN / USER:
PASSWORD / PIN:
NOTES / RECOVERY QUESTION / PASS PHRASE / HINT:

TITEL:
WEB ADDRESS:
LOGIN / USER:
PASSWORD / PIN:
NOTES / RECOVERY QUESTION / PASS PHRASE / HINT:

TITEL:

WEB ADDRESS:

LOGIN / USER:

PASSWORD / PIN:

NOTES / RECOVERY QUESTION / PASS PHRASE / HINT:

TITEL:

WEB ADDRESS:

LOGIN / USER:

PASSWORD / PIN:

NOTES / RECOVERY QUESTION / PASS PHRASE / HINT:

TITEL:

WEB ADDRESS:

LOGIN / USER:

PASSWORD / PIN:

NOTES / RECOVERY QUESTION / PASS PHRASE / HINT:

TITEL:
WEB ADDRESS:
LOGIN / USER:
PASSWORD / PIN:
NOTES / RECOVERY QUESTION / PASS PHRASE / HINT:

TITEL:
WEB ADDRESS:
LOGIN / USER:
PASSWORD / PIN:
NOTES / RECOVERY QUESTION / PASS PHRASE / HINT:

TITEL:
WEB ADDRESS:
LOGIN / USER:
PASSWORD / PIN:
NOTES / RECOVERY QUESTION / PASS PHRASE / HINT:

TITEL:

WEB ADDRESS:

LOGIN / USER:

PASSWORD / PIN:

NOTES / RECOVERY QUESTION / PASS PHRASE / HINT:

TITEL:

WEB ADDRESS:

LOGIN / USER:

PASSWORD / PIN:

NOTES / RECOVERY QUESTION / PASS PHRASE / HINT:

TITEL:

WEB ADDRESS:

LOGIN / USER:

PASSWORD / PIN:

NOTES / RECOVERY QUESTION / PASS PHRASE / HINT:

TITEL:
WEB ADDRESS:
LOGIN / USER:
PASSWORD / PIN:
NOTES / RECOVERY QUESTION / PASS PHRASE / HINT:

TITEL:
WEB ADDRESS:
LOGIN / USER:
PASSWORD / PIN:
NOTES / RECOVERY QUESTION / PASS PHRASE / HINT:

TITEL:
WEB ADDRESS:
LOGIN / USER:
PASSWORD / PIN:
NOTES / RECOVERY QUESTION / PASS PHRASE / HINT:

TITEL:

WEB ADDRESS:

LOGIN / USER:

PASSWORD / PIN:

NOTES / RECOVERY QUESTION / PASS PHRASE / HINT:

TITEL:

WEB ADDRESS:

LOGIN / USER:

PASSWORD / PIN:

NOTES / RECOVERY QUESTION / PASS PHRASE / HINT:

TITEL:

WEB ADDRESS:

LOGIN / USER:

PASSWORD / PIN:

NOTES / RECOVERY QUESTION / PASS PHRASE / HINT:

TITEL:
WEB ADDRESS:
LOGIN / USER:
PASSWORD / PIN:
NOTES / RECOVERY QUESTION / PASS PHRASE / HINT:

TITEL:
WEB ADDRESS:
LOGIN / USER:
PASSWORD / PIN:
NOTES / RECOVERY QUESTION / PASS PHRASE / HINT:

TITEL:
WEB ADDRESS:
LOGIN / USER:
PASSWORD / PIN:
NOTES / RECOVERY QUESTION / PASS PHRASE / HINT:

TITEL:

WEB ADDRESS:

LOGIN / USER:

PASSWORD / PIN:

NOTES / RECOVERY QUESTION / PASS PHRASE / HINT:

TITEL:

WEB ADDRESS:

LOGIN / USER:

PASSWORD / PIN:

NOTES / RECOVERY QUESTION / PASS PHRASE / HINT:

TITEL:

WEB ADDRESS:

LOGIN / USER:

PASSWORD / PIN:

NOTES / RECOVERY QUESTION / PASS PHRASE / HINT:

TITEL:
WEB ADDRESS:
LOGIN / USER:
PASSWORD / PIN:
NOTES / RECOVERY QUESTION / PASS PHRASE / HINT:

TITEL:
WEB ADDRESS:
LOGIN / USER:
PASSWORD / PIN:
NOTES / RECOVERY QUESTION / PASS PHRASE / HINT:

TITEL:
WEB ADDRESS:
LOGIN / USER:
PASSWORD / PIN:
NOTES / RECOVERY QUESTION / PASS PHRASE / HINT:

TITEL:
WEB ADDRESS:
LOGIN / USER:
PASSWORD / PIN:
NOTES / RECOVERY QUESTION / PASS PHRASE / HINT:

TITEL:
WEB ADDRESS:
LOGIN / USER:
PASSWORD / PIN:
NOTES / RECOVERY QUESTION / PASS PHRASE / HINT:

TITEL:
WEB ADDRESS:
LOGIN / USER:
PASSWORD / PIN:
NOTES / RECOVERY QUESTION / PASS PHRASE / HINT:

TITEL:

WEB ADDRESS:

LOGIN / USER:

PASSWORD / PIN:

NOTES / RECOVERY QUESTION / PASS PHRASE / HINT:

TITEL:

WEB ADDRESS:

LOGIN / USER:

PASSWORD / PIN:

NOTES / RECOVERY QUESTION / PASS PHRASE / HINT:

TITEL:

WEB ADDRESS:

LOGIN / USER:

PASSWORD / PIN:

NOTES / RECOVERY QUESTION / PASS PHRASE / HINT:

TITEL:

WEB ADDRESS:

LOGIN / USER:

PASSWORD / PIN:

NOTES / RECOVERY QUESTION / PASS PHRASE / HINT:

TITEL:

WEB ADDRESS:

LOGIN / USER:

PASSWORD / PIN:

NOTES / RECOVERY QUESTION / PASS PHRASE / HINT:

TITEL:

WEB ADDRESS:

LOGIN / USER:

PASSWORD / PIN:

NOTES / RECOVERY QUESTION / PASS PHRASE / HINT:

TITEL:

WEB ADDRESS:

LOGIN / USER:

PASSWORD / PIN:

NOTES / RECOVERY QUESTION / PASS PHRASE / HINT:

TITEL:

WEB ADDRESS:

LOGIN / USER:

PASSWORD / PIN:

NOTES / RECOVERY QUESTION / PASS PHRASE / HINT:

TITEL:

WEB ADDRESS:

LOGIN / USER:

PASSWORD / PIN:

NOTES / RECOVERY QUESTION / PASS PHRASE / HINT:

TITEL:
WEB ADDRESS:
LOGIN / USER:
PASSWORD / PIN:
NOTES / RECOVERY QUESTION / PASS PHRASE / HINT:

TITEL:
WEB ADDRESS:
LOGIN / USER:
PASSWORD / PIN:
NOTES / RECOVERY QUESTION / PASS PHRASE / HINT:

TITEL:
WEB ADDRESS:
LOGIN / USER:
PASSWORD / PIN:
NOTES / RECOVERY QUESTION / PASS PHRASE / HINT:

TITEL:
WEB ADDRESS:
LOGIN / USER:
PASSWORD / PIN:
NOTES / RECOVERY QUESTION / PASS PHRASE / HINT:

TITEL:
WEB ADDRESS:
LOGIN / USER:
PASSWORD / PIN:
NOTES / RECOVERY QUESTION / PASS PHRASE / HINT:

TITEL:
WEB ADDRESS:
LOGIN / USER:
PASSWORD / PIN:
NOTES / RECOVERY QUESTION / PASS PHRASE / HINT:

TITEL:
WEB ADDRESS:
LOGIN / USER:
PASSWORD / PIN:
NOTES / RECOVERY QUESTION / PASS PHRASE / HINT:

TITEL:
WEB ADDRESS:
LOGIN / USER:
PASSWORD / PIN:
NOTES / RECOVERY QUESTION / PASS PHRASE / HINT:

TITEL:
WEB ADDRESS:
LOGIN / USER:
PASSWORD / PIN:
NOTES / RECOVERY QUESTION / PASS PHRASE / HINT:

TITEL:
WEB ADDRESS:
LOGIN / USER:
PASSWORD / PIN:
NOTES / RECOVERY QUESTION / PASS PHRASE / HINT:

TITEL:
WEB ADDRESS:
LOGIN / USER:
PASSWORD / PIN:
NOTES / RECOVERY QUESTION / PASS PHRASE / HINT:

TITEL:
WEB ADDRESS:
LOGIN / USER:
PASSWORD / PIN:
NOTES / RECOVERY QUESTION / PASS PHRASE / HINT:

TITEL:

WEB ADDRESS:

LOGIN / USER:

PASSWORD / PIN:

NOTES / RECOVERY QUESTION / PASS PHRASE / HINT:

TITEL:

WEB ADDRESS:

LOGIN / USER:

PASSWORD / PIN:

NOTES / RECOVERY QUESTION / PASS PHRASE / HINT:

TITEL:

WEB ADDRESS:

LOGIN / USER:

PASSWORD / PIN:

NOTES / RECOVERY QUESTION / PASS PHRASE / HINT:

TITEL:
WEB ADDRESS:
LOGIN / USER:
PASSWORD / PIN:
NOTES / RECOVERY QUESTION / PASS PHRASE / HINT:

TITEL:
WEB ADDRESS:
LOGIN / USER:
PASSWORD / PIN:
NOTES / RECOVERY QUESTION / PASS PHRASE / HINT:

TITEL:
WEB ADDRESS:
LOGIN / USER:
PASSWORD / PIN:
NOTES / RECOVERY QUESTION / PASS PHRASE / HINT:

TITEL:

WEB ADDRESS:

LOGIN / USER:

PASSWORD / PIN:

NOTES / RECOVERY QUESTION / PASS PHRASE / HINT:

TITEL:

WEB ADDRESS:

LOGIN / USER:

PASSWORD / PIN:

NOTES / RECOVERY QUESTION / PASS PHRASE / HINT:

TITEL:

WEB ADDRESS:

LOGIN / USER:

PASSWORD / PIN:

NOTES / RECOVERY QUESTION / PASS PHRASE / HINT:

TITEL:
WEB ADDRESS:
LOGIN / USER:
PASSWORD / PIN:
NOTES / RECOVERY QUESTION / PASS PHRASE / HINT:

TITEL:
WEB ADDRESS:
LOGIN / USER:
PASSWORD / PIN:
NOTES / RECOVERY QUESTION / PASS PHRASE / HINT:

TITEL:
WEB ADDRESS:
LOGIN / USER:
PASSWORD / PIN:
NOTES / RECOVERY QUESTION / PASS PHRASE / HINT:

TITEL:

WEB ADDRESS:

LOGIN / USER:

PASSWORD / PIN:

NOTES / RECOVERY QUESTION / PASS PHRASE / HINT:

TITEL:

WEB ADDRESS:

LOGIN / USER:

PASSWORD / PIN:

NOTES / RECOVERY QUESTION / PASS PHRASE / HINT:

TITEL:

WEB ADDRESS:

LOGIN / USER:

PASSWORD / PIN:

NOTES / RECOVERY QUESTION / PASS PHRASE / HINT:

TITEL:
WEB ADDRESS:
LOGIN / USER:
PASSWORD / PIN:
NOTES / RECOVERY QUESTION / PASS PHRASE / HINT:

TITEL:
WEB ADDRESS:
LOGIN / USER:
PASSWORD / PIN:
NOTES / RECOVERY QUESTION / PASS PHRASE / HINT:

TITEL:
WEB ADDRESS:
LOGIN / USER:
PASSWORD / PIN:
NOTES / RECOVERY QUESTION / PASS PHRASE / HINT:

TITEL:
WEB ADDRESS:
LOGIN / USER:
PASSWORD / PIN:
NOTES / RECOVERY QUESTION / PASS PHRASE / HINT:

TITEL:
WEB ADDRESS:
LOGIN / USER:
PASSWORD / PIN:
NOTES / RECOVERY QUESTION / PASS PHRASE / HINT:

TITEL:
WEB ADDRESS:
LOGIN / USER:
PASSWORD / PIN:
NOTES / RECOVERY QUESTION / PASS PHRASE / HINT:

TITEL:

WEB ADDRESS:

LOGIN / USER:

PASSWORD / PIN:

NOTES / RECOVERY QUESTION / PASS PHRASE / HINT:

TITEL:

WEB ADDRESS:

LOGIN / USER:

PASSWORD / PIN:

NOTES / RECOVERY QUESTION / PASS PHRASE / HINT:

TITEL:

WEB ADDRESS:

LOGIN / USER:

PASSWORD / PIN:

NOTES / RECOVERY QUESTION / PASS PHRASE / HINT:

TITEL:
WEB ADDRESS:
LOGIN / USER:
PASSWORD / PIN:
NOTES / RECOVERY QUESTION / PASS PHRASE / HINT:

TITEL:
WEB ADDRESS:
LOGIN / USER:
PASSWORD / PIN:
NOTES / RECOVERY QUESTION / PASS PHRASE / HINT:

TITEL:
WEB ADDRESS:
LOGIN / USER:
PASSWORD / PIN:
NOTES / RECOVERY QUESTION / PASS PHRASE / HINT:

TITEL:
WEB ADDRESS:
LOGIN / USER:
PASSWORD / PIN:
NOTES / RECOVERY QUESTION / PASS PHRASE / HINT:

TITEL:
WEB ADDRESS:
LOGIN / USER:
PASSWORD / PIN:
NOTES / RECOVERY QUESTION / PASS PHRASE / HINT:

TITEL:
WEB ADDRESS:
LOGIN / USER:
PASSWORD / PIN:
NOTES / RECOVERY QUESTION / PASS PHRASE / HINT:

TITEL:

WEB ADDRESS:

LOGIN / USER:

PASSWORD / PIN:

NOTES / RECOVERY QUESTION / PASS PHRASE / HINT:

TITEL:

WEB ADDRESS:

LOGIN / USER:

PASSWORD / PIN:

NOTES / RECOVERY QUESTION / PASS PHRASE / HINT:

TITEL:

WEB ADDRESS:

LOGIN / USER:

PASSWORD / PIN:

NOTES / RECOVERY QUESTION / PASS PHRASE / HINT:

TITEL:
WEB ADDRESS:
LOGIN / USER:
PASSWORD / PIN:
NOTES / RECOVERY QUESTION / PASS PHRASE / HINT:

TITEL:
WEB ADDRESS:
LOGIN / USER:
PASSWORD / PIN:
NOTES / RECOVERY QUESTION / PASS PHRASE / HINT:

TITEL:
WEB ADDRESS:
LOGIN / USER:
PASSWORD / PIN:
NOTES / RECOVERY QUESTION / PASS PHRASE / HINT:

TITEL:
WEB ADDRESS:
LOGIN / USER:
PASSWORD / PIN:
NOTES / RECOVERY QUESTION / PASS PHRASE / HINT:

TITEL:
WEB ADDRESS:
LOGIN / USER:
PASSWORD / PIN:
NOTES / RECOVERY QUESTION / PASS PHRASE / HINT:

TITEL:
WEB ADDRESS:
LOGIN / USER:
PASSWORD / PIN:
NOTES / RECOVERY QUESTION / PASS PHRASE / HINT:

TITEL:
WEB ADDRESS:
LOGIN / USER:
PASSWORD / PIN:
NOTES / RECOVERY QUESTION / PASS PHRASE / HINT:

TITEL:
WEB ADDRESS:
LOGIN / USER:
PASSWORD / PIN:
NOTES / RECOVERY QUESTION / PASS PHRASE / HINT:

TITEL:
WEB ADDRESS:
LOGIN / USER:
PASSWORD / PIN:
NOTES / RECOVERY QUESTION / PASS PHRASE / HINT:

TITEL:

WEB ADDRESS:

LOGIN / USER:

PASSWORD / PIN:

NOTES / RECOVERY QUESTION / PASS PHRASE / HINT:

TITEL:

WEB ADDRESS:

LOGIN / USER:

PASSWORD / PIN:

NOTES / RECOVERY QUESTION / PASS PHRASE / HINT:

TITEL:

WEB ADDRESS:

LOGIN / USER:

PASSWORD / PIN:

NOTES / RECOVERY QUESTION / PASS PHRASE / HINT:

TITEL:

WEB ADDRESS:

LOGIN / USER:

PASSWORD / PIN:

NOTES / RECOVERY QUESTION / PASS PHRASE / HINT:

TITEL:

WEB ADDRESS:

LOGIN / USER:

PASSWORD / PIN:

NOTES / RECOVERY QUESTION / PASS PHRASE / HINT:

TITEL:

WEB ADDRESS:

LOGIN / USER:

PASSWORD / PIN:

NOTES / RECOVERY QUESTION / PASS PHRASE / HINT:

Titel: Email (Private):
eMail Server Type:
Server (incoming):
Server (outgoing):
Login / User:
Password / Pin:

Titel: Email:
eMail Server Type:
Server (incoming):
Server (outgoing):
Login / User:
Password / Pin:

Titel: Internet Service Provider (ISP) Support
Name ISP:
Web address ISP:
Customer Number:
Hotline Customer Support:
Email Customer Support:
Web Address Customer Support:

TITEL: EMAIL (PRIVATE):
EMAIL SERVER TYPE:
SERVER (INCOMING):
SERVER (OUTGOING):
LOGIN / USER:
PASSWORD / PIN:

TITEL: EMAIL:
EMAIL SERVER TYPE:
SERVER (INCOMING):
SERVER (OUTGOING):
LOGIN / USER:
PASSWORD / PIN:

TITEL: INTERNET SERVICE PROVIDER (ISP) SUPPORT
NAME ISP:
WEB ADDRESS ISP:
CUSTOMER NUMBER:
HOTLINE CUSTOMER SUPPORT:
EMAIL CUSTOMER SUPPORT:
WEB ADDRESS CUSTOMER SUPPORT:

TITEL: BROADBAND MODEM	TITEL: CONFIGURATION WLAN
MODEL:	HOST NAME:
FACTORY NR.:	DOMAIN NAME:
MAC ADDRESS:	SUBNET MASK:
URL/IP ADMIN:	GATEWAY:
IP WAN:	DNS (PRIMARY):
LOGIN/USER:	DNS (SECONDARY):
PASSWORD:	

TITEL: ROUTER / WIRELESS ACCESS POINT
MODEL:
FACTORY NUMBER:
FACTORY SETTING ADMIN IP:
FACTORY SETTING USERNAME:
FACTORY SETTING PASSWORD:
USER DEFINED ADMIN URL /IP:
USER DEFINED USERNAME:
USER DEFINED PASSWORD:

TITEL: WIRELESS-LAN
SSID / NAME WLAN NETWORK:
SECURITY TYPE:
ENCRYPTION TYPE:
SHARED KEY (WPA):
HINT (PASSPHRASE WEP):

TITEL: BROADBAND MODEM	TITEL: CONFIGURATION WLAN
MODEL:	HOST NAME:
FACTORY NR.:	DOMAIN NAME:
MAC ADDRESS:	SUBNET MASK:
URL/IP ADMIN:	GATEWAY:
IP WAN:	DNS (PRIMARY):
LOGIN/USER:	DNS (SECONDARY):
PASSWORD:	

TITEL: ROUTER / WIRELESS ACCESS POINT
MODEL:
FACTORY NUMBER:
FACTORY SETTING ADMIN IP:
FACTORY SETTING USERNAME:
FACTORY SETTING PASSWORD:
USER DEFINED ADMIN URL /IP:
USER DEFINED USERNAME:
USER DEFINED PASSWORD:

TITEL: WIRELESS-LAN
SSID / NAME WLAN NETWORK:
SECURITY TYPE:
ENCRYPTION TYPE:
SHARED KEY (WPA):
HINT (PASSPHRASE WEP):

NOTES:

NOTES:

NOTES: